MORNING GLORY

PENHALIGON'S SCENTED TREASURY
OF SPRING VERSE AND PROSE

For Alice Anne

EDITED BY
SHEILA PICKLES

LONDON MCMXCII

INTRODUCTION

Dear Reader,

When the snowdrops push their green spears through the earth I know that spring has arrived, and each year I think what a miracle it is. No matter how long the winter, how hard the frost or how deep the snow, Nature triumphs. No season is awaited so eagerly or welcomed so warmly as spring. Our great poets have celebrated the season with some of their finest lines, and I have selected a few of my favourites for your pleasure.

Spring is the start of the calendar year, the season of hope the promise of new life. Each year I am astonished by the wealth of flowers the season gives us: the subtlety of the wild primroses and violets, the rich palette of crocus in the parks, tall soldier tulips and proud trumpeting daffodils and narcissi. When the buds open and the lime green leaves start to sprout in my garden I am filled with excitement and anticipation and am always reminded of Mole in *The Wind in the Willows* spring-cleaning his little home, then flinging down his brush and bolting out into the sunshine to play with his friends.

Spring is the season when we shed our cloaks and make our plans for the year, be it for the garden, our homes, our lives. I hope this small book will encourage you to take a few moments thinking of what you would like the year to bring for you and that all your plans will be realized.

Sheila Pickles, Canonbury, London, 1992

POT-POURRI

I RECENTLY read an article in which the writer said that she appreciated pot-pourri so much more in the knowledge that it was twice-touched. The flowers are first enjoyed whilst blooming in the garden, and then valued all year round when they are being dried. They are best picked early in the day before the heat of the sun is upon them, as Friar Lawrence told us in Romeo and Juliet:

> 'Now, ere the sun advance his burning eye
> The day to cheer and night's dank dew to dry,
> I must up-fill this osier cage of ours
> With baleful weeds and precious-juiced flowers.'

The newly-picked flowers and herbs should be hung up to dry and left until they are crisp. Then they may be broken up and tossed with aromatic oils. If the mix is for a big bowl, I like to decorate the top with sprigs of herbs or large flower heads and select the colours according to the decor of the room. I also choose the scent according to the season and more especially depending on where it is going to lie. Old white linen can be useful to make lavender bags, which look pretty tied with ribbons to a bed-post or a door knob. I currently have a spicy pot-pourri bag inside my wardrobe door, which delicately scents my winter suits and which I will change for one scented with perhaps lily or rose in the spring. A scented bag placed under a guests pillow is a welcome surprise and may help them to sleep after a long journey. A sachet slipped into a trunk of linens will lie quietly there for years and the sheets will come out smelling fresh and crisp a decade later. I even have a friend who throws lavender or pot-pourri over the floor, vacuums it up and each time she cleans the scent in the bag perfumes the room.

The uses for a spring pot-pourri are many and varied; I hope that you will take some of my ideas and make them your own.

THE MAY GARLAND

*T*HE May garland was all that survived there of the old May Day festivities. The maypole and the May games and May dances in which whole parishes had joined had long been forgotten. Beyond giving flowers for the garland and pointing out how things should be done and telling how they had been done in their own young days, the older people took no part in the revels.

From *Lark Rise to Candleford* by Flora Thompson, 1876-1947

MAIDEN MAY

MAIDEN May sat in her bower,
In her blush rose bower in flower,
Sweet of scent;
Sat and dreamed away an hour,
Half content, half uncontent.

'Why should rose blossoms be born,
Tender blossoms, on a thorn
Tho' so sweet?
Never a thorn besets the corn
Scentless in its strength complete.

'Why are roses all so frail,
At the mercy of a gale,
Of a breath?
Yet so sweet and perfect pale,
Still so sweet in life and death.'

Maiden May sat in her bower,
In her blush rose bower in flower,
Where a linnet
Made one bristling branch the tower
For her nest and young ones in it.

Christina Rossetti, 1830-1894

An Encounter On The Seine

*W*ITHOUT knowing how or why I found myself on the banks of the Seine. Steamers were going past on their way to Suresnes and I was suddenly seized by an indescribable longing to go running through the woods.

The deck of the *Mouche* was crowded with passengers, for the first sunny day draws you out of doors in spite of yourself, and everyone is on the move, coming and going, and chattering with his neighbour.

My neighbour was a girl – a little working-girl no doubt – with a charm that was entirely Parisian. She had a sweet little face with a fair complexion and golden hair clustering round her temples like curls of light. Dancing in the breeze, her hair rippled down to her ears and the nape of her neck, and then, lower still, turned into down so fine and light that I could scarcely see it but felt an irresistible longing to cover it with kisses. . . .

I was just about to speak to her when somebody touched me on the shoulder. I turned round in surprise and saw an ordinary-looking man, neither young nor old, who was gazing at me sadly.

'I should like to have a word with you,' he said.

I pulled a face, and no doubt he noticed, for he added: 'It's a matter of importance.'

I got up and followed him to the other end of the boat.

'Monsieur,' he continued, 'when winter comes with cold, and rain and snow, your doctor says to you whenever he sees you: "Keep your feet warm, and beware of chills, colds, bronchitis and pleurisy." So you take all sorts of precautions: you wear flannel underwear, thick overcoats and heavy shoes. And even then you sometimes find yourself bed-ridden for a couple of months. But when spring returns with its leaves and flowers, its warm relaxing breezes, and its country scents which fill you with a vague disquiet and inexplicable emotions, there is nobody to say to you: "Monsieur, beware of love!"

From *In the Spring* by Guy de Maupassant

Inviting The Influence
Of A Young Lady
Upon The Opening Year

You wear the morning like your dress
And are with mastery crown'd;
When as you walk your loveliness
Goes shining all around:
Upon your secret, smiling way
Such new contents were found,
The Dancing Loves made holiday
On that delightful ground.
Then summon April forth, and send
Commandment through the flowers;
About our woods your grace extend,
A queen of careless hours.
For O! not Vera veil'd in rain,
Nor Dian's sacred Ring,
With all her royal nymphs in train
Could so lead on the Spring.

Hilaire Belloc, 1870-1953

THE SENSITIVE PLANT

A SENSITIVE Plant in a garden grew,
And the young winds fed it with silver dew,
And it opened its fan-like leaves to the light,
And closed them beneath the kisses of night.

And the Spring arose on the garden fair,
And the Spirit of Love fell everywhere;
And each flower and herb on Earth's dark breast
Rose from the dreams of its wintry rest.

But none ever trembled and panted with bliss
In the garden, the field, or the wilderness,
Like a doe in the noontide with love's sweet want,
As the companionless Sensitive Plant.

The snowdrop, and then the violet,
Arose from the ground with warm rain wet,
And their breath was mixed with fresh odour, sent
From the turf, like the voice and the instrument.

P. B. Shelley, 1792-1822

BLOSSOM

$\mathcal{S}$IPPING weak tea with lemon in it, Jolyon gazed through the leaves of the old oak tree at that view which had appeared to him desirable for thirty-two years. The tree beneath which he sat seemed not a day older! So young, the little leaves of brownish gold; so old, the whitey-grey-green of its thick rough trunk. A tree of memories, which would live on hundreds of years yet, unless some barbarian cut it down – would see old England out at the pace things were going! . . .

From where he sat he could see a cluster of apple trees in blossom. Nothing in Nature moved him so much as fruit trees in blossom; and his heart ached suddenly because he might never see them flower again. Spring! Decidedly no man ought to have to die while his heart was still young enough to love beauty! Blackbirds sang recklessly in the shrubbery, swallows were flying high, the leaves above him glistened; and over the fields was every imaginable tint of early foliage, burnished by the level sunlight, away to where the distant 'smoke-bush' blue was trailed along the horizon. Irene's flowers in their narrow beds had startling individuality that evening, little deep assertions of gay life. Only Chinese and Japanese painters, and perhaps Leonardo, had known how to get that startling little ego into each painted flower, and bird, and beast – the ego, yet the sense of species, the universality of life as well. They were the fellows! 'I've made nothing that will live!' thought Jolyon; 'I've been an amateur – a mere lover, not a creater. Still, I shall leave Jon behind me when I go.' What luck that the boy had not been caught by that ghastly war! He might so easily have been killed, like poor Jolly twenty years ago out in the Transvaal. Jon would do something some day – if the Age didn't spoil him – an imaginative chap! His whim to take up farming was but a bit of sentiment, and about as likely to last. And just then he saw them coming up the field: Irene and the boy, walking from the station, with their arms linked. And getting up, he strolled down through the new rose garden to meet them. . . .

From *To Let* by John Galsworthy, 1867-1933

COWSLIPS

I THINK there is no scent on earth to come up to that of the cowslips; I fancy primroses are sickly, but cowslips are the very embodiment of spring and I do not like to see them made into wine and puddings as they are in these parts of England. A cowslip pudding sounds ideal, but it is mostly suet and imagination. Now a cowslip ball is a delight and Marjorie naturally has her fill of the sweet and dainty things. She never sees them faded or dead as long as the flowers last, for when she is in bed to-day's balls are neatly cremated; we tell her the fairies called for them for their children and the next day's balls are always fresh. I think if I were ninety I should feel young making a cowslip ball, and if Marjorie and Steeple and the cowslips were combined I could not recollect my age, of that I am sure.

From *Leaves of a Garden* by Miss Panton, c. 1910

The Weather Of New England

*G*ENTLEMEN: I reverently believe that the Maker who made us all, makes everything in New England – but the weather. I don't know who makes that, but I think it must be raw apprentices in the Weather Clerk's factory, who experiment and learn how in New England, for board and clothes, and then are promoted to make weather for countries that require a good article, and will take their custom elsewhere if they don't get it. There is a sumptuous variety about the New England weather that compels the stranger's admiration – and regret. The weather is always doing something there; always attending strictly to business; always getting up new designs and trying them on the people to see how they will go. But it gets through more business in spring than in any other season. In the spring I have counted one hundred and thirty six different kinds of weather inside of four and twenty hours. It was I that made the fame and fortune of that man that had that marvelous collection of weather on exhibition at the Centennial that so astounded the foreigners. He was going to travel all over the world and get specimens from all the climes. I said, 'Don't you do it; you come to New England on a favorable spring day.' I told him what we could do, in the way of style, variety, and quantity. Well, he came, and he made his collection in four days. As to variety – why, he confessed that he got hundreds of kinds of weather that he had never heard of before. And as to quantity – well, after he had picked out and discarded all that was blemished in any way, he not only had weather enough, but weather to spare; weather to hire out; weather to sell; to deposit; weather to invest; weather to give to the poor.

The people of New England are by nature patient and forbearing; but there are some things which they will not stand. Every year they kill a lot of poets for writing about 'Beautiful Spring.' These are generally casual visitors, who bring their notions of spring from somewhere else, and cannot, of course, know how the natives feel about spring. And so, the first thing they know, the opportunity to inquire how they feel has permanently gone by.

From *Annual Dinner Speech to New England Society of New York* by Mark Twain, 1835-1910

FISHING

*T*HEY were on their way to the Round Pool – that wonderful
pool, which the floods had made a long while ago: no one
knew how deep it was; and it was mysterious, too, that it should
be almost a perfect round, framed in with willows and tall reeds,
so that the water was only to be seen when you got close to the
brink. The sight of the old favourite spot always heightened Tom's
good-humour, and he spoke to Maggie in the most amicable
whispers, as he opened the precious basket, and prepared their

tackle. He threw her line for her, and put the rod into her hand. Maggie thought it probable that the small fish would come to her hook, and the large ones to Tom's. But she had forgotten all about the fish, and was looking dreamily at the glassy water, when Tom said, in a loud whisper, 'Look, look, Maggie!' and came running to prevent her from snatching her line away.

Maggie was frightened lest she had been doing something wrong, as usual, but presently Tom drew out her line and brought a large tench bouncing on the grass.

Tom was excited.

'Oh, Magsie! you little duck! Empty the basket.'

Maggie was not conscious of unusual merit, but it was enough that Tom called her Magsie, and was pleased with her. There was nothing to mar her delight in the whispers and the dreamy silences, when she listened to the light dipping sounds of the rising fish, and the gentle rustling, as if the willows and the reeds and the water had their happy whisperings also. Maggie thought it would make a very nice heaven to sit by the pool in that way, and never be scolded. She never knew she had a bite till Tom told her, but she liked fishing very much.

It was one of their happy mornings. They trotted along and sat down together, with no thought that life would ever change much for them; they would only get bigger and not go to school, and it would always be like the holidays; they would always live together and be fond of each other. And the mill with its booming – the great chestnut-tree under which they played at houses – their own little river, the Ripple, where the banks seemed like home, and Tom was always seeing the water-rats, while Maggie gathered the purple plumy tops of the reeds, which she forgot and dropped afterwards – above all, the great Floss, along which they wandered with a sense of travel, to see the rushing spring-tide, the awful Eagre, come up like a hungry monster, or to see the Great Ash which had once wailed and groaned like a man – these things would always be just the same to them.

From *The Mill on the Floss* by George Eliot, 1819-1880

A U B A D E

HARK! hark! the lark at heaven's gate sings,
And Phœbus 'gins arise,
His steeds to water at those springs
On chaliced flowers that lies;
And winking Mary-buds begin
To ope their golden eyes:
With everything that pretty bin,
My lady sweet, arise!
Arise, arise!

William Shakespeare, 1564-1616

A GENTLE SEASON

*B*UT the privations, or rather the hardships, of Lowood lessened. Spring drew on – she was indeed already come; the frosts of winter had ceased; its snows were melted, its cutting winds ameliorated. My wretched feet, flayed and swollen to lameness by the sharp air of January, began to heal and subside under the gentler breathings of April; the nights and mornings no longer by their Canadian temperature froze the very blood in our veins; we could now endure the playhour passed in the garden;

sometimes on a sunny day it began even to be pleasant and genial, and a greenness grew over those brown beds, which, freshening daily, suggested the thought that Hope traversed them at night, and left each morning brighter traces of her steps. Flowers peeped out among the leaves: snowdrops, crocuses, purple auriculas, and golden-eyed pansies. On Thursday afternoons (half-holidays) we now took walks, and found still sweeter flowers opening by the wayside under the hedges.

April advanced to May – a bright serene May it was; days of blue sky, placid sunshine, and soft western or southern gales filled up its duration. And now vegetation matured with vigour; Lowood shook loose its tresses; it became all green, all flowers; its great elm, ash, and oak skeletons were restored to majestic life; woodland plants sprang up profusely in its recesses; unnumbered varieties of moss filled its hollows, and it made a strange ground-sunshine out of the wealth of its wild primrose plants: I have seen their pale gold gleam in overshadowed spots like scatterings of the sweetest lustre.

From *Jane Eyre* by Charlotte Bronte, 1816-1855

THE LETTER

*E*LIZABETH awoke the next morning to the same thoughts and meditations which had at length closed her eyes. She could not yet recover from the surprise of what had happened; it was impossible to think of anything else, and totally indisposed for employment, she resolved soon after breakfast to indulge herself in air and exercise. She was proceeding directly to her favourite walk, when the recollection of Mr Darcy's sometimes coming there stopped her, and instead of entering the park, she turned up the lane, which led her farther from the turnpike road. The park paling was still the boundary on one side, and she soon passed out of the gates into the ground.

After walking two or three times along that part of the lane, she was tempted, by the pleasantness of the morning, to stop at the gates and look into the park. The five weeks which she had now passed in Kent, had made a great difference in the country, and every day was adding to the verdure of the early trees. She was on the point of continuing her walk, when she caught a glimpse of a gentleman within the sort of grove which edged the park; he was moving that way; and fearful of its being Mr Darcy, she was directly retreating. But the person who advanced, was now near enough to see her, and stepping forward with eagerness, pronounced her name. She had turned away, but on hearing herself called, though in a voice which proved it to be Mr Darcy, she moved again towards the gate. He had by that time reached it also, and holding out a letter, which she instinctively took, said with a look of haughty composure, 'I have been walking in the grove some time in the hope of meeting you. Will you do me the honour of reading that letter?' – And then, with a slight bow, turned again into the plantation, and was soon out of sight.

From *Pride and Prejudice* by Jane Austen, 1775-1817

WASHINGTON SQUARE

*S*HE continued to walk down the Fifth Avenue, without noticing the cross-streets, and after a while became conscious that she was approaching Washington Square. By this time she had also definitely reasoned it out that Basil Ransom and Henry Burrage could not both capture Miss Tarrant, that therefore there could not be two dangers, but only one; that this was a good deal gained, and that it behoved her to determine which peril had most reality, in order that she might deal with that one only. She held her way to the Square, which, as all the world knows, is of great extent and open to the encircling street. The trees and grass-plots had begun to bud and sprout, the fountains splashed in the sunshine, the children of the quarter, both the dingier types from the south side, who played games that required much chalking of the paved walks, and much sprawling and crouching there, under the feet of passers, and the little curled and feathered people who drove their hoops under the eyes of French nursemaids – all the infant population filled the vernal air with small sounds which had a crude, tender quality, like the leaves and the thin herbage. Olive wandered through the place, and ended by sitting down on one of the continuous benches. It was a long time since she had done anything so vague, so wasteful. There were a dozen things which, as she was staying over in New York, she ought to do; but she forgot them, or, if she thought of them, felt that they were now of no moment. She remained in her place an hour, brooding, tremulous, turning over and over certain thoughts. It seemed to her that she was face to face with a crisis of her destiny, and that she must not shrink from seeing it exactly as it was. Before she rose to return to Tenth Street she had made up her mind that there was no menace so great as the menace of Basil Ransom; she had accepted in thought any arrangement which would deliver her from that. If the Burrages were to take Verena they would take her from Olive immeasurably less than he would do; it was from him, from him they would take her most. She walked back to her boarding-house, and the servant who admitted her said, in answer to her inquiry as to whether Verena were at home, that Miss Tarrant had gone out with the gentleman who called in the morning, and had not yet come in. Olive stood staring; the clock in the hall marked three.

From *The Bostonians* by Henry James, 1843-1916

SOAMES' PROMISE

THERE had been rain the night before – a spring rain, and the earth smelt of sap and wild grasses. The warm, soft breeze swung the leaves and the golden buds of the old oak-tree, and in the sunshine the blackbirds were whistling their hearts out.

It was such a spring day as breathes into a man an ineffable yearning, a painful sweetness, a longing that makes him stand motionless, looking at the leaves of grass, and fling out his arms to embrace he knows not what. The earth gave forth a fainting warmth, stealing up through the chilly garment in which winter had wrapped her. It was her long caress of invitation, to draw men down to lie within her arms, to roll their bodies on her, and put their lips to her breast.

On just such a day as this Soames had got from Irene the promise he had asked her for so often. Seated on the fallen trunk of a tree, he had promised for the twentieth time that if their marriage were not a success, she should be as free as if she had never married him!

'Do you swear it?' she had said. A few days back she had reminded him of that oath. He had answered: 'Nonsense! I couldn't have sworn any such think!' By some awkward fatality he remembered it now. What queer things men would swear for the sake of women! He would have sworn it at any time to gain her! He would swear it now, if thereby he could touch her – but nobody could touch her, as she was cold-hearted!

And memories crowded on him with the fresh, sweet savour of the spring wind – memories of his courtship.

From *The Man of Property* by John Galsworthy, 1867-1933

CORINNA'S GOING A-MAYING

GET up, get up for shame! The blooming morn
Upon her wings presents the god unshorn.
          See how Aurora throws her fair
          Fresh-quilted colours through the air:

          Get up, sweet slug-a-bed, and see
          The dew bespangling herb and tree!
Each flower has wept and bow'd toward the east
Above an hour since, yet you not drest;
          Nay! not so much as out of bed?
          When all the birds have matins said
          And sung their thankful hymns, 'tis sin,
          Nay, profanation, to keep in,
Whereas a thousand virgins on this day
Spring sooner than the lark, to fetch in May.

          Rise and put on your foliage, and be seen
To come forth, like the spring-time, fresh and green,
          And sweet as Flora. Take no care
          For jewels for your gown or hair:
          Fear not; the leaves will strew
          Gems in abundance upon you:
Besides, the childhood of the day has kept,
·Against you come, some orient pearls unwept,
          Come, and receive them while the light
          Hangs on the dew-locks of the night:
          And Titan on the eastern hill
          Retires himself, or else stands still
Till you come forth! Wash, dress, be brief in praying:
Few beads are best when once we go a-Maying.

Robert Herrick, 1591-1674

AN UNKINDLY MAY

A SHEPHERD stands by a gate in a white smock-frock:
He holds the gate ajar, intently counting his flock.

The sour spring wind is blurting boisterous-wise,
And bears on it dirty clouds across the skies;
Plantation timbers creak like rusty cranes,
And pigeons and rooks, dishevelled by late rains,
Are like gaunt vultures, sodden and unkempt,
And song-birds do not end what they attempt:
The buds have tried to open, but quite failing
Have pinched themselves together in their quailing.
The sun frowns whitely in eye-trying flaps
Through passing cloud-holes, mimicking audible taps.
'Nature, you're not commendable to-day!'
I think. 'Better to-morrow!' she seems to say.

That shepherd still stands in that white smock-frock
Unnoting all things save the counting his flock.

Thomas Hardy, 1840-1928

A Provençal Spring

$\mathscr{L}$ittle Manon was approaching her tenth year. She was all golden, with sea blue eyes too big for her face, and hair so thick that her mother could hardly extract the oak leaves, pine needles, or bramble twigs from it without a pair of scissors.

The wind of the hills, the friendship of the trees, and the silence of the lonely places had fashioned her into a little wild animal, as light and lively as a fox. Her great love was Baptistine,

whom she admired like somebody from a fairy story, and the Piedmontese adored her. Every morning they watched their goats together on the plateaux of the garigue. Baptistine taught her how to look after animals, the art of setting traps, and the thousand secrets of the hills; at first she did this in incomprehensible French, illustrated with gestures and grimaces; but after some weeks the little girl was able to understand, and then to speak, the rough patois of Piedmont. She would go down to Les Romarins mounted on the galloping she-ass, uttering cries of victory; and in the pouches of the pack she brought wild food: bloodred mushrooms, big pine kernels, spongy morels, snails fed on thyme, and blackbirds perfumed with myrtle, or thrushes gorged on juniper berries.

At first she was a little ashamed when she threw dead birds on the table, and refused to eat them.

One evening her father gravely declared, while sliding a row of lard-covered ortolans from a skewer:

'One always gets soft about the misfortunes of little birds, because they fly and go tweet-tweet. But remember they are ferocious animals that massacre minute living creatures in order to eat them. . . .

'And as for old maids who weep for innocent blackbirds or kind finches, I've noticed they never weep when they see a lamb cutlet; even when they see them on burning charcoal, it's the cutlet that does the weeping!'

And he started to chew a piece of toast, golden with the sizzling grease of fat ortolans. She took one in her turn, and her tender scruples faded away.

From *Manon des Sources* by Marcel Pagnol, 1895-1974

LUNCHEON ON THE GRASS

'My lord has ordered the char-a-banc, and is going to drive us all to Chart, where we will lunch,' said Lady St. Jerome; ''tis a curious place, and was planted only seventy years ago by my Lord's grandfather, entirely with spruce firs, but with so much care and skill, giving each plant and tree ample distance, that they have risen to the noblest proportions, with all their green branches far-spreading on the ground like huge fans.'

It was only a drive of three or four miles entirely in the park. This was a district that had been added to the ancient enclosure; a striking scene. It was a forest of firs, but quite unlike such as might be met with in the north of Europe or of America. Every tree was perfect, huge and complete, and full of massy grace. Nothing else was permitted to grow there except juniper, of which there were abounding and wondrous groups, green and spiral; the whole contrasting with the tall brown fern of which there were quantities about cut for the deer.

The turf was dry and mossy, and the air pleasant. It was a balmy day. They sat down by the great trees, the servants opened the luncheon baskets, which were a present from Balmoral. Lady St. Jerome was seldom seen to greater advantage than distributing her viands under such circumstances. Never was such gay and graceful hospitality. Lothair was quite fascinated as she playfully thrust a paper of lobster-sandwiches into his hand, and enjoined Monsignore Catesby to fill his tumbler with Chablis.

From *Lothair* by Benjamin Disraeli, 1804-1881

SPRING

NOTHING is so beautiful as spring –
When weeds, in wheels, shoot long and lovely and lush;
Thrush's eggs look little low heavens, and thrush
Through the echoing timber does so rinse and wring
The ear, it strikes like lightnings to hear him sing;
The glassy peartree leaves and blooms, they brush
The descending blue; that blue is all in a rush
With richness; the racing lambs too have fair their fling.

What is all this juice and all this joy?
A strain of the earth's sweet being in the beginning
In Eden garden. – Have, get, before it cloy,
Before it cloud, Christ, lord, and sour with sinning,
Innocent mind and Mayday in girl and boy,
Most, O maid's child, thy choice and worthy the winning.

Gerard Manley Hopkins, 1844-1889

THE PRIMROSE

ASKE me why I send you here
This sweet *Infanta* of the yeare?
Aske me why I send to you
This Primrose, thus bepearl'd with dew?
I will whisper to your eares,
The sweets of Love are mixt with tears.

Ask me why this flower do's show
So yellow-green, and sickly too?
Ask me why the stalk is weak
And bending (yet it does not break)?
I will answer, these discover
What fainting hopes are in a Lover.

Robert Herrick, 1591-1674

THE TWENTY-SECOND OF FEBRUARY, 1940

*T*HE hard weather has gone for the moment, and the first deceptive day of Spring arrived with so warm a rush as to make us believe it would be succeeded by many others. Of course with our reason we know that this is unlikely. We know that a bit of February is still to come and the whole of March, frequently one of the most unpleasant months in the calendar. Yet it is difficult to be prudent and sceptical when the first sunlight one has seen for many weeks wakes one between the curtains and makes one leap from bed to find a very different kind of day awaiting one outside. Warm air is surprising after the shivering cold one has learned to expect. It is surprising to find that one wants to throw off one's coat instead of dragging it closely round one. How delightful to be free of the heavy coat! How delightful to walk unhampered, even if only for one day! How delightful to enjoy in a platitudinous way the simple pleasures of the first suggestion of spring: the birds singing once more, the earth soft to the tread after the stiffness of frost, the evidence of things beginning again to love and bud and grow.

We Britons are perhaps specially sensitive to such movements of the seasons, since our seasons melt and merge into one another more elastically than the more violently demarcated seasons of stronger climates. Our seasons interchange their character in a way unknown to the extremes of North or South. Thus the citizen of Leningrad knows that the spring will not arrive till the middle of May and arranges his existence and his mind to suit that necessity; he does not expect the spring and so is not disappointed when he does not get it somewhere in the middle of February; the inhabitant of Shiraz, on the other hand, would be extremely indignant if his spring suddenly reverted to winter. We have learnt to be more tolerant. We are grateful for the one warm day coming in the midst of our tribulations, and with our usual happy-go-lucky optimism assume at once that the warm happy days have arrived to last.

From *Country Notes in Wartime* by Vita Sackville-West, 1892-1962

TO DAFFODILS

FAIR daffodils, we weep to see
You haste away so soon;
As yet the early-rising sun
Has not attain'd his noon.
Stay, stay
Until the hasting day
Has run
But to the evensong;
And, having pray'd together, we
Will go with you along.

We have short time to stay, as you,
We have as short a spring;
As quick a growth to meet decay,
As you, or anything.
We die
As your hours do, and dry
Away
Like to the summer's rain;
Or as the pearls of morning's dew,
Ne'er to be found again.

Robert Herrick, 1591-1674

PARTING FROM THE
WINTER STOVE

On the fifth day after the rise of Spring,
Everywhere the season's gracious attitudes!
The white sun gradually lengthening its course,
The blue-grey clouds hanging as though they would fall;
The last icicle breaking into splinters of jade:
The new stems marshalling red sprouts.
The things I meet are all full of gladness;
It is not only *I* who love the spring.
To welcome the flowers I stand in the back garden;
To enjoy the sunlight I sit under the front eaves.
Yet still in my heart there lingers one regret;
Soon I shall part with the flame of my red stove!

Chinese poem, anon., AD 822

S P R I N G

WHEN daisies pied and violets blue,
And lady-smocks all silver-white,
And cuckoo-buds of yellow hue
Do paint the meadows with delight,
The cuckoo then, on every tree,
Mocks married men; for thus sings he,
Cuckoo!
Cuckoo, cuckoo! – O word of fear,
Unpleasing to a married ear!

When shepherds pipe on oaten straws,
And merry larks are ploughmen's clocks,
When turtles tread, and rooks, and daws,
And maidens bleach their summer smocks
The cuckoo then, on every tree,
Mocks married men; for thus sings he,
Cuckoo!
Cuckoo, cuckoo! – O word of fear,
Unpleasing to a married ear!

William Shakespeare, 1564-1616

A SPRING RESOLUTION

*I*T WAS now early spring – the time of going to grass with the sheep, when they have the first feed of the meadows, before these are laid up for mowing. The winds, which had been blowing east for several weeks, had veered to the southward, and the middle of spring had come abruptly – almost without a beginning. It was that period in the vernal quarter when we may suppose the Dryads to be waking for the season. The vegetable world begins to move and swell and the saps to rise, till in the completest silence of lone gardens and trackless plantations, where everything seems helpless and still after the bond and slavery of frost, there are bustlings, strainings, united thrusts, and pulls-all-together, in comparison with which the powerful tugs of cranes and pulleys in a noisy city are but pigmy-efforts.

Boldwood, looking into the distant meadows, saw there three figures. They were those of Miss Everdene, Shepherd Oak, and Cainy Ball.

When Bathsheba's figure shone upon the farmer's eyes it lighted him up as the moon lights up a great tower. A man's body is as the shell, or the tablet, of his soul, as he is reserved or ingenuous, overflowing or self-contained. There was a change in Boldwood's exterior from its former impassibleness; and his face showed that he was now living outside his defences for the first time, and with a fearful sense of exposure. It is the usual experience of strong natures when they love.

At last he arrived at a conclusion. It was to go across and inquire boldly of her.

From *Far From the Madding Crowd* by Thomas Hardy, 1840-1928

TO SPRING

O THOU with dewy locks, who lookest down
Through the clear windows of the morning, turn
Thine angel eyes upon our western isle,
Which in full choir hails thy approach, O Spring!

The hills tell one another, and the listening
Valleys hear; all our longing eyes are turn'd
Up to thy bright pavilions: issue forth
And let thy holy feet visit our clime!

Come o'er the eastern hills, and let our winds
Kiss thy perfumèd garments; let us taste
Thy morn and evening breath; scatter thy pearls
Upon our lovesick land that mourns for thee.

O deck her forth with thy fair fingers; pour
Thy soft kisses on her bosom; and put
Thy golden crown upon her languish'd head,
Whose modest tresses are bound up for thee.

William Blake, 1757-1827

EARLIEST SPRING

TOSSING his mane of snows in wildest eddies and tangles,
Lion-like March cometh in, hoarse, with tempestuous breath,
Through all the moaning chimneys, and 'thwart all the hollows and angles
Round the shuddering house, threating of winter and death.

But in my heart I feel the life of the wood and the meadow
Thrilling the pulses that own kindred with fibres that lift
Bud and blade to the sunward, within the inscrutable shadow,
Deep in the oak's chill core, under the gathering drift.

Nay, to earth's life in mine some prescience, or dream, or desire
(How shall I name it aright?) comes for a moment and goes –
Rapture of life ineffable, perfect – as if in the brier,
Leafless there by my door, trembled a sense of the rose.

William Dean Howells, 1837-1920

Beeny Cliff

O the opal and the sapphire of that wandering western sea,
And the woman riding high above with bright hair flapping free –
The woman whom I loved so, and who loyally loved me.

The pale mews plained below us, and the waves seemed far away
In a nether sky, engrossed in saying their ceaseless babbling say,
As we laughed light-heartedly aloft on that clear-sunned March day.

A little cloud then cloaked us, and there flew an irised rain,
And the Atlantic dyed its levels with a dull misfeatured stain,
And then the sun burst out again, and purples prinked the main.

Still in all its chasmal beauty bulks old Beeny to the sky,
And shall she and I not go there once again now March is nigh
And the sweet things said in that March say anew there by and by?

What if still in chasmal beauty looms that wild weird western shore,
The woman now is – elsewhere – whom the ambling pony bore,
And nor knows nor cares for Beeny, and will laugh there never-more.

Thomas Hardy, 1840-1928

APRIL À LA MODE

*Y*OUNG girls, but only young girls, have entirely discarded long dresses for dancing. Long dresses, however, are still worn by ladies, who do not dance – or, at the utmost, dance in quadrilles, when the long dress, if well worn, is more graceful than short skirts. With short dresses, laced-up shoes, as high as Polish boots, are invariably worn.

Ball dresses are made of almost every material, of every colour, and style. Everything is allowed, so long as it looks pretty, and is becoming to the wearer. Fashion has now but one aim, that of making every lady look her best, whatever her complexion, features, or figure may be. Thus, velvet may be mixed with satin, silk, brocade, tulle and gauze, or each may be worn by itself. This liberty of colour and material, allows a past season's dress to be renewed.

From *Parisian Gossip, The Lady's Treasury*, 1880

NEW LIFE

*Y*ET it was spring, and the bluebells were coming in the wood, and the leaf-buds on the hazels were opening like the spatter of green rain. How terrible it was that it should be spring, and everything cold-hearted, cold-hearted. Only the hens, fluffed so wonderfully on the eggs, were warm with their hot, brooding female bodies! Connie felt herself living on the brink of fainting all the time.

Then, one day, a lovely sunny day with great tufts of primroses under the hazels, and many violets dotting the paths, she came in the afternoon to the coops and there was one tiny, tiny perky chicken tinily prancing round in front of a coop, and the mother hen clucking in terror. The slim little chick was greyish brown with dark markings, and it was the most alive little spark of a creature in seven kingdoms at that moment. Connie crouched to watch in a sort of ecstasy. Life, life! Pure, sparky, fearless new life! New life! So tiny and so utterly without fear! Even when it scampered a little, scrambling into the coop again, and disappeared under the hen's feathers in answer to the mother hen's wild alarm-cries, it was not really frightened, it took it as a game, the game of living. For in a moment a tiny sharp head was poking through the gold-brown feathers of the hen, and eyeing the Cosmos.

Connie was fascinated. And at the same time, never had she felt so acutely the agony of her own female forlornness. It was becoming unbearable.

She had only one desire now, to go to the clearing in the wood. The rest was a kind of painful dream.

From *Lady Chatterly's Lover* by D. H. Lawrence, 1885-1930

HOME-THOUGHTS,
FROM ABROAD

O TO be in England
Now that April's there,
And whoever wakes in England
Sees, some morning, unaware,
That the lowest boughs and the brushwood sheaf
Round the elm-tree bole are in tiny leaf,
While the chaffinch sings on the orchard bough
In England – now!

And after April, when May follows,
And the whitethroat builds, and all the swallows!
Hark, where my blossom'd pear-tree in the hedge
Leans to the field and scatters on the clover
Blossoms and dewdrops – at the bent spray's edge –
That's the wise thrush; he sings each song twice over,

Lest you should think he never could recapture
The first fine careless rapture!
And though the fields look rough with hoary dew,
All will be gay when noontide wakes anew
The buttercups, the little children's dower
– Far brighter than this gaudy melon-flower!

Robert Browning, 1812-1889

Amell Fine Art, Stockholm, Sweden/Courtesy Medici Society:
p24/25 *Ejord in Summer*: Paul Gustaf Fischer.

Bridgeman Art Library:
p5 *The Walk* (Argenteuil): Claude Monet/Christie's, London; p8/9 *May Day*: James Hayllar/Christie's, London; p13 *Richmond Bridge*: James Jacques Tissot/Ronald T Lewis Collection, USA; p14 *In the Field*: Dame Laura Knight © Reproduced by permission of the Curtis Brown Group; p18 *Springtime*: Alexander Mann/Whitford & Hughes; p19 *Lily of the Valley* and *Cowslips*: Ursula Hodgson/Private Collection; p21 *A Breath of Fresh Air*: Daniel Hernandez/Whitford & Hughes; p22 *The Young Fisherman*: Thomas Blacklock/Bonham's, London; p26 *Young Lady Sketching in Landscape*: Henry Le Jeune/Christopher Wood Gallery, London; p33 *A Sketch of a Faraway Look*: Herman Richir/Bonham's, London; p36 *Shepherd Bringing Home his Flock*: John Robert Keitley/Graham Reed Fine Art, York; p37 *Shepherd with a Lamb*: Sir George Clausen/Cecil Higgins Art Gallery, Bedford; p38 *Provençal Spring*: Henry Herbert La Thangue/Bradford City Art Gallery and Museums; p40 *A Birthday Picnic*: Arthur Hughes/Forbes Magazine Collection, NY; p47 *The Kintai Bridge in Springtime*: Hasui/Private Collection; p48 *Wild Violets*: J. Le Moyne de Morgues/V&A; p53 *The Circlet of White Flowers*: Elizabeth Sonrel/Whitford & Hughes; p54 *Cheerful Spring from my Window*: George Frederick Watts/Fine Art Society; p55 *By the Sea*: Povl Steffensen/Christie's London; 56/57 *The White Ball*: Joseph Marius Avy/Musée de Petit Palais, Paris; p58 *Young Woman in Green*: James William Glacken/Private Collection; p59 *Five Chickens*: Mabel Townesend/City of York Art Gallery, York; p61 *On the Balcony*: Ester Borough Johnson/Whitford & Hughes.

Fine Art Photographic Archive:
p15 *Violets and Snowdrops*: Anon; p17 *In the Orchard*: Lucien Frank; p27 *Daisies, Primroses and Violets with a Bird's Nest*: C H Slater; p28 *Seclusion*, 1920: Edmund Blair Leighton; p42 *April in the Meadows*: William H Bartlett; p43 *Daydreaming*: Dewey Bates; p45 *Girl in an Orchard*: Harry Foskey; p46 *Reading*: Janet Archer; p63 *Dreams*: Sir Frederick William Burton.

Fine Arts Society: p11 *Apple Blossom*: Sir George Clausen/Private Collection.

Phillips Collection, Washington, DC: p30 *Washington Arch in Spring*, 1890: Childe Hassam.

Royal Academy of Arts, London: p7 *Violets for Perfume*: Henry Herbert La Thangue; p50 *The Lass of Richmond Hill*: George Dunlop Leslie.

Sotheby's, London: p49 *La Primavera*: Henry Ryland/Private Collection.

Tyne & Wear Museums: p3 *In the Spring*: © Harold Knight/Reproduced by permission of The Curtis Brown Group, London.

Yale University Art Gallery: p34/35 May Day Morning: Edwin Austin Abbey/The Edwin Austin Abbey Memorial Collection.

Cover: *Dreams*: Sir Frederick William Burton/Fine Art Photographic Archive.

Morning Glory

This evocative floral scent was created by Penhaligon's in 1991 to represent the spring in the quartet of the four seasons. Spring flowers tend to bring colour to the garden rather than perfume, so we took blossom to represent the season and allowed the lily to dominate the fresh green scent.

The pot-pourri contains three shades of delphiniums, marjoram, blue achillea, pink anaphalis, bay leaves, French and English lavender and bayberry.

PAVILION

First published in Great Britain in 1992 by
PAVILION BOOKS LIMITED
196 Shaftesbury Avenue
London WC2H 8JL

p8 *Larkrise to Candleford* by Flora Thompson, reproduced by kind
permission of Oxford University Press, Oxford.
p14 *Inviting the Influence of a Young Lady Upon the Opening Year* by Hilaire
Belloc, reproduced by kind permission of Peters, Fraser and Dunlop, London.
p38/39 *Manon des Sources* by Marcel Pagnol. Reproduced in Britain and
Canada by kind permission of André Deutsch, London; and in the USA by
North Point Press, California.
p44 *The Twenty-Second of February, 1940* from *Country Notes in Wartime* by
Vita Sackville-West, reproduced by kind permission of the Curtis Brown Ltd, London.
p47 *Parting from the Winter Stove* anonymous, from *Chinese Poems*, compiled
and translated by Arthur Walley (Unwin Paperbacks, 1961). Reproduced by
kind permission of HarperCollins Publishers Ltd, London.

Designed by Andrew Barron & Collis Clements Associates
Original design concept by Bernard Higton
Picture research by Lynda Marshall

A CIP catalogue record for this book is available
from the British Library

ISBN 1-85145-857-3

Printed in Great Britain by Bath Press Colourbooks, Glasgow

10 9 8 7 6 5 4 3 2 1

For more information about Penhaligon's perfumes,
please telephone London (071) 880 2050 or write to:
PENHALIGON'S
41 Wellington Street
Covent Garden
London WC2